DANZA
for Strings / pour Cordes

Duration : approx. 7 minutes

VACLAV NELHYBEL

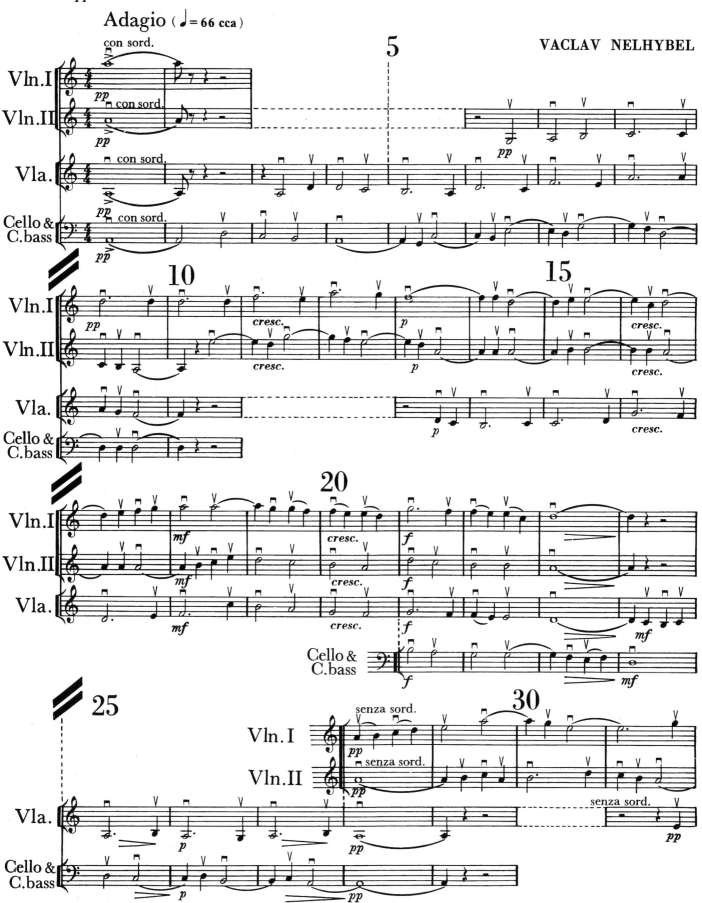

Copyright © 1971 by E. C. KERBY, Ltd.
International Copyright Secured

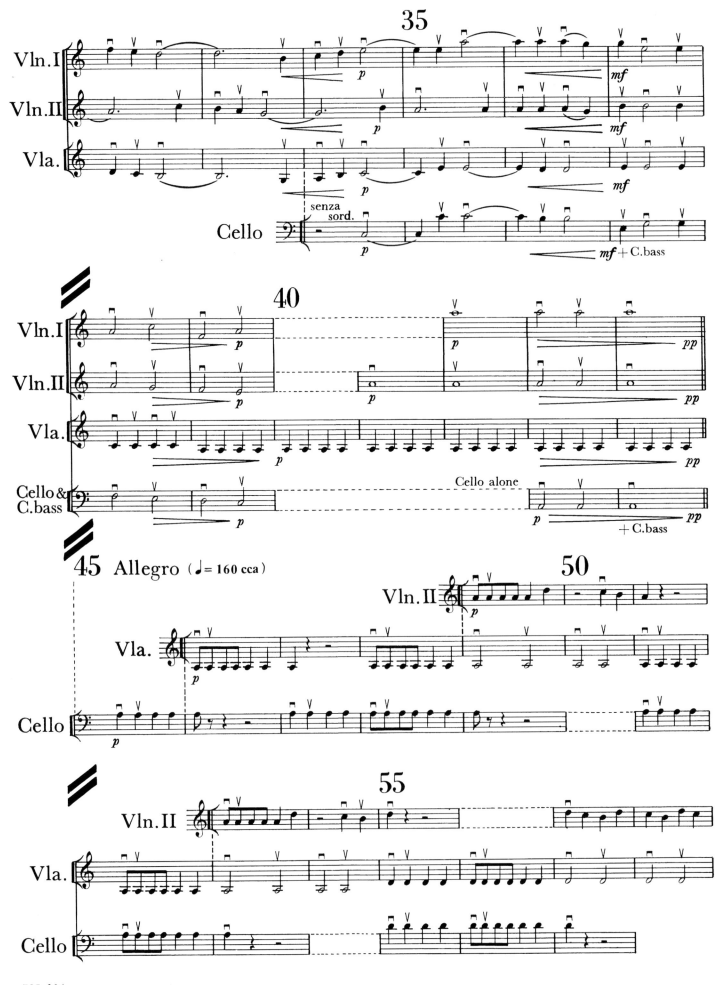

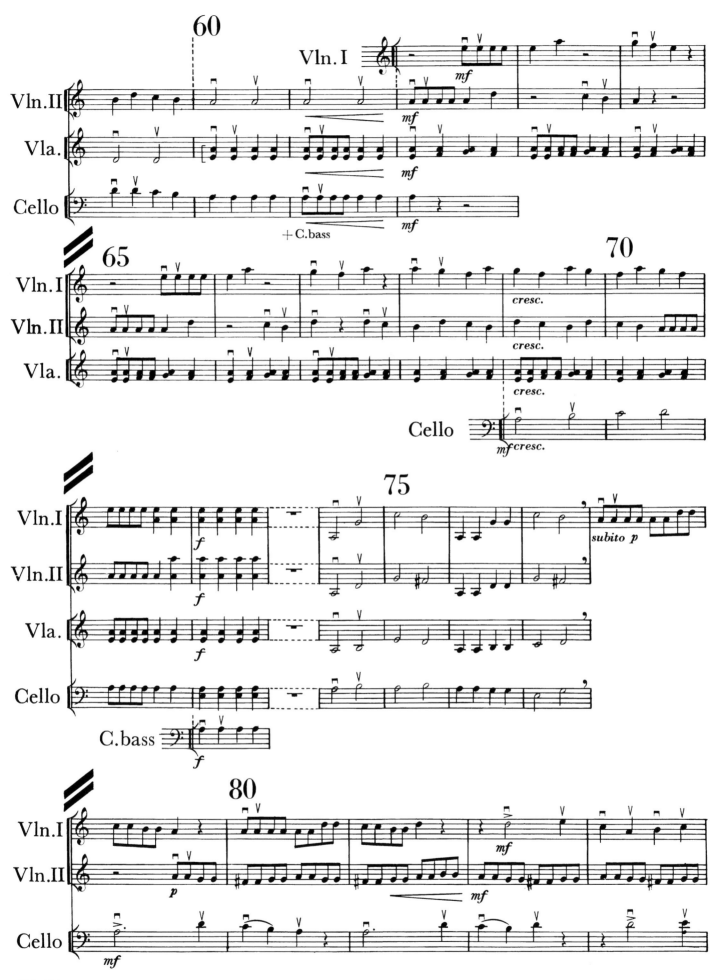

735-004

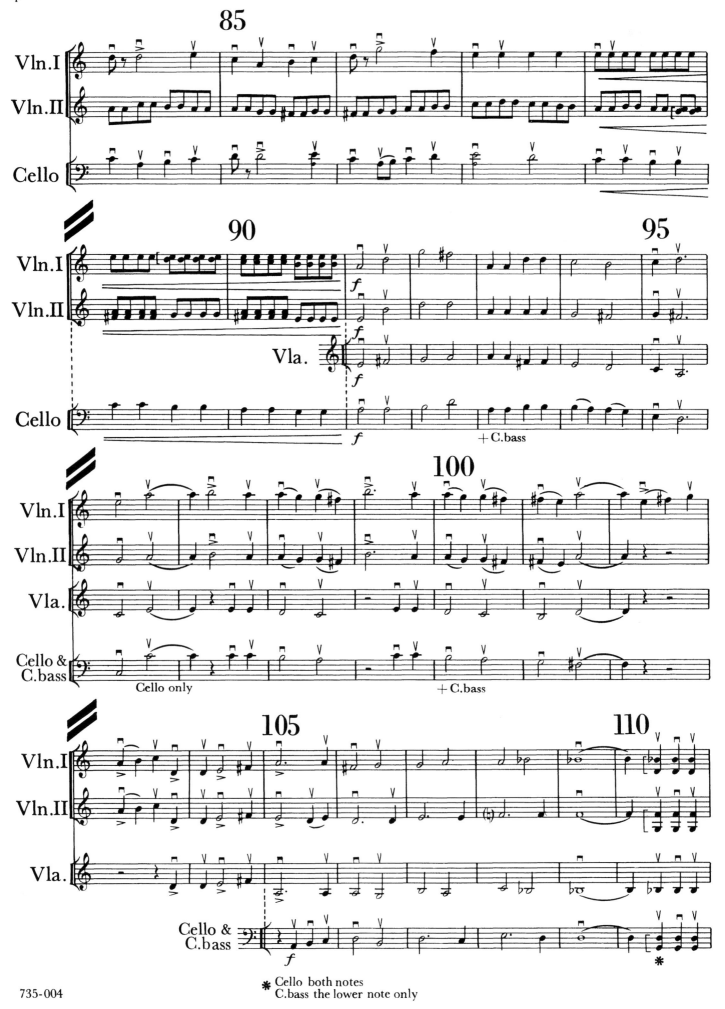

* Cello both notes
C.bass the lower note only

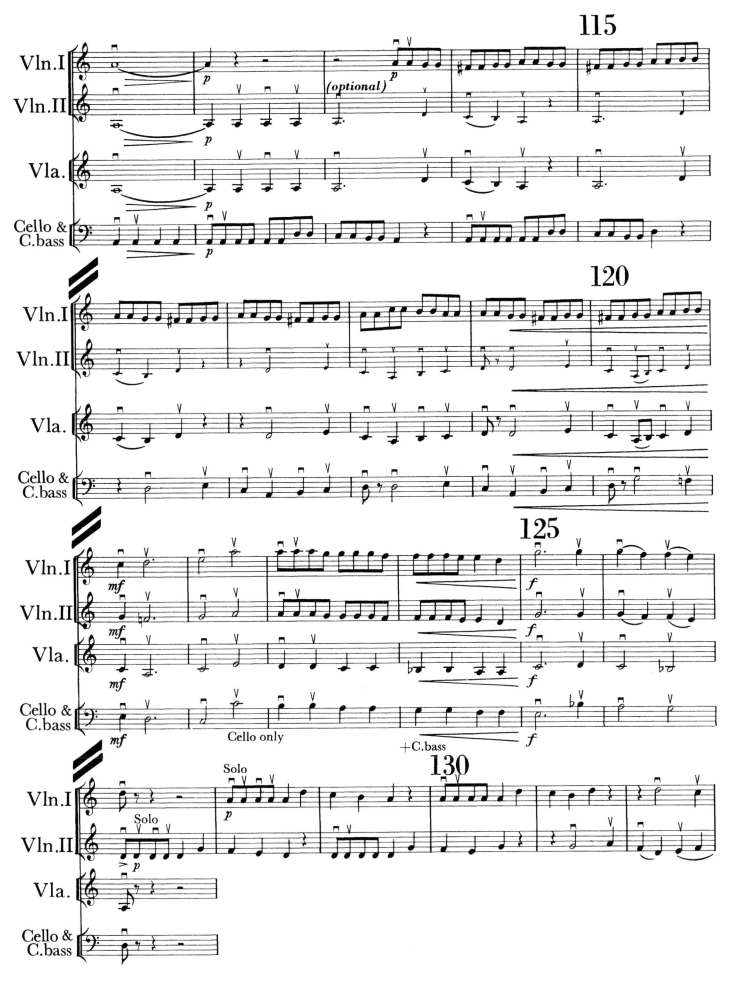

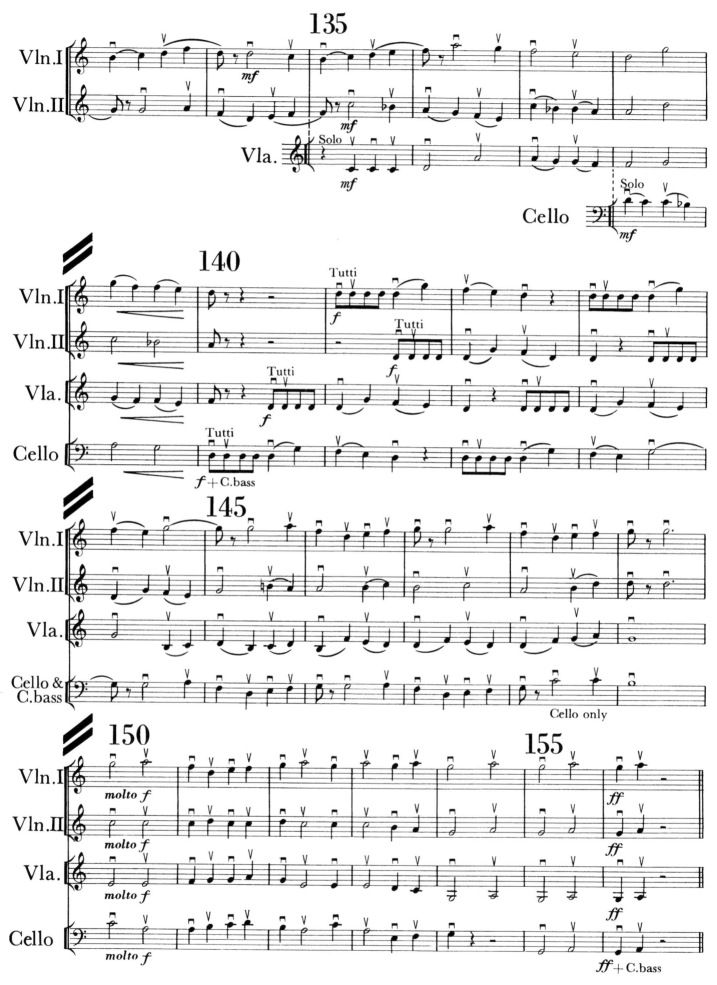

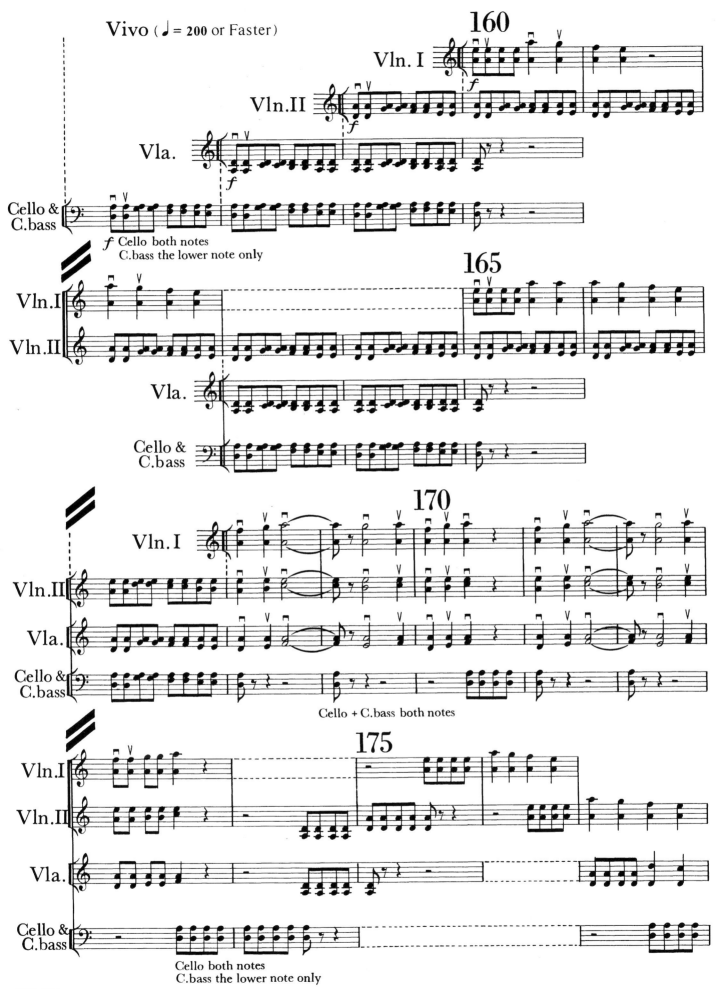

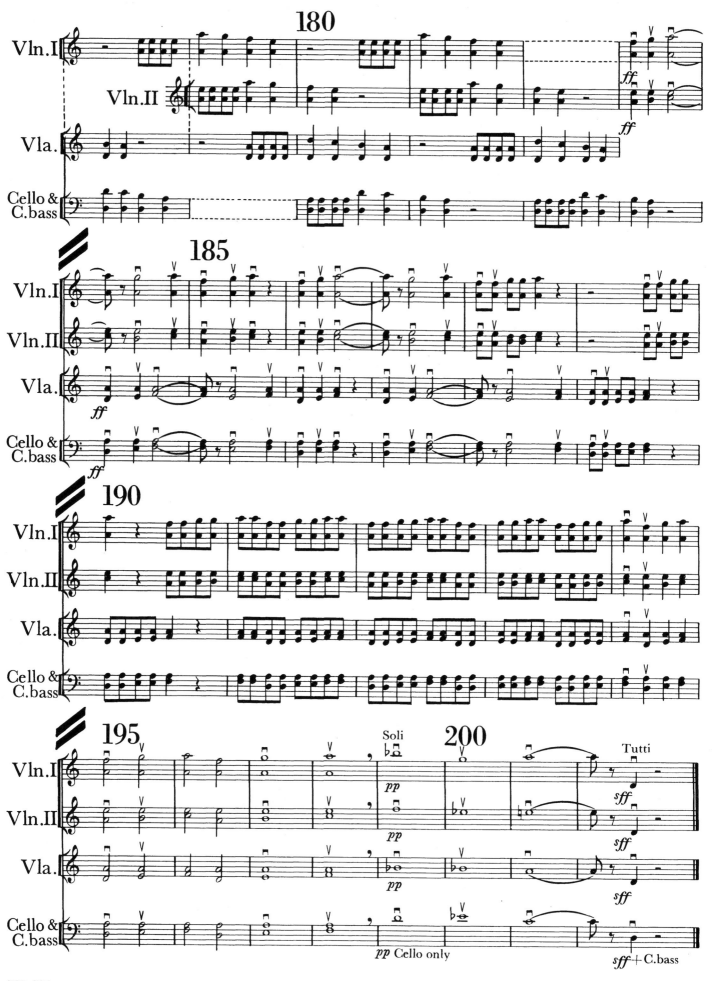